LifeChange

A NAVPRESS BIBLE STUDY SERIES

*A life-changing
encounter with God's Word*

FORGIVENESS

*Followers of Jesus model His posture of
forgiveness, acceptance, and reconciliation.*

NavPress

A NavPress resource published in alliance
with Tyndale House Publishers

T0003233

CONTENTS

HOW TO USE THIS STUDY

Objectives

The topical guides in the LifeChange series of Bible studies cover important topics from the Bible. Although the LifeChange guides vary with the topics they explore, they share some common goals:

1. to help readers grasp what key passages in the Bible say about the topic;

2. to provide readers with explanatory notes, word definitions, historical background, and cross-references so that the only other reference they need is the Bible;

3. to teach readers how to let God's Word transform them into Christ's image;

4. to provide small groups with a tool that will enhance group discussion of each passage and topic; and

5. to write each session so that advance preparation for group members is strongly encouraged but not required.

Each lesson in this study is designed to take forty-five minutes to complete.

Overview and Details

The study begins with an overview of forgiveness. The key to interpretation for each part of this study is content (what is the referenced passage *about?*), and the key to context is purpose (what is the author's *aim* for the passage as it relates to the overall topic?). Each lesson of the study explores an aspect of forgiveness with a corresponding passage from the Bible.

Kinds of Questions

Bible study provides different lenses and perspectives through which to engage the Scripture: observe (what does the passage *say*?), interpret (what does the passage *mean*?), and apply (how does this truth *affect* my life?). Some of the "how" and "why" questions will take some creative thinking, even prayer, to answer. Some are opinion questions without clear-cut right answers; these will lend themselves to discussions and side studies.

Don't let your study become an exercise in knowledge alone. Treat the passage as God's Word, and stay in dialogue with Him as you study. Pray, *Lord, what do You want me to see here?, Father, why is this true?*, and *Lord, how does this apply to my life?*

It is important that you write down your answers. The act of writing clarifies your thinking and helps you to remember what you're learning.

Study Aids

Throughout the guide, there are study aids that provide background information on the passage, insights from commentaries, and word studies. These aids are included in the guide to help you interpret the Bible without needing to use other, outside resources. Still, if you're interested in exploring further, the full resources are listed in the endnotes.

Scripture Versions

Unless otherwise indicated, the Bible quotations in this guide are from the New International Version of the Bible. The other versions cited are *The Message* and the *New English Translation*.

Use any translation you like for study—or preferably more than one. Ideally you would have on hand a good, modern translation such as the New International Version, the English Standard Version, the New Living Translation, or the Christian Standard Bible. A paraphrase such as *The Message* is not accurate enough for study, but it can be helpful for comparison or devotional reading.

Memorizing and Meditating

A psalmist wrote, "I have hidden your word in my heart that I might not sin against you" (Psalm 119:11). If you write down a verse or passage that challenges or encourages you and reflect on it often for a week or more, you will find it beginning to affect your motives and actions. We forget quickly what we read once; we remember what we ponder.

When you find a significant verse or passage, you might copy it onto a card to keep with you. Set aside five minutes each day just to think about what the passage might mean in your life. Recite it to yourself, exploring its meaning. Then, return to the passage as often as you can during the day for a brief review. You will soon find it coming to mind spontaneously.

For Group Study

A group of four to ten people allows the richest discussions, but you can adapt this guide for other-sized groups. It will suit a wide range of group types, such as home Bible studies, growth groups, youth groups, and workplace Bible studies. Both new and experienced Bible students, and new and mature Christians, will benefit from the guide. You can omit or leave for later any questions you find too easy or too hard. The guide is intended to lead a group through one lesson per meeting. This guide is formatted so you will be able to discuss each of the questions at length. Be sure to make time at each discussion for members to ask about anything they didn't understand.

Each member should prepare for a meeting by writing answers for all the background and discussion questions to be covered. Application will be very difficult, however, without private thought and prayer.

Two reasons for studying in a group are accountability and support. When each member commits in front of the rest to seek growth in an area of life, you can pray for one another, listen jointly for God's guidance, help one another resist temptation, assure each other that each person's growth matters to you, use the group to practice spiritual principles, and so on. Pray about one another's commitments and needs at most meetings. If you wish, you can spend the first few minutes of each meeting sharing any results from applications prompted by previous lessons and discuss new applications toward the end of the meeting. Follow your time of sharing with prayer for these and other needs.

If you write down what others have shared, you are more likely to remember to pray for them during the week, ask about what they shared at the next meeting, and notice answered prayers. You might want to get a notebook for prayer requests and discussion notes.

Taking notes during discussion will help you remember to follow up on ideas, stay on the subject, and have clarity on an issue. But don't let note-taking keep you from participating.

Some best practices for groups:

1. If possible, come to the group discussion prepared. The more each group member knows about the passage and the questions being asked, the better your discussion will be.

2. Realize that the group leader will not be teaching from the passage but instead will be facilitating your discussion. Therefore, it is important for each group member to participate so that everyone can contribute to what you learn as a group.

3. Try to stick to the passage covered in the session and the specific questions in the study guide.

4. Listen attentively to the other members of the group when they are sharing their thoughts about the passage. Also, realize that most of the questions are open-ended, allowing for more than one answer.

5. Be careful not to dominate the discussion—especially if you are the leader. Allow time for everyone to share their thoughts and ideas.

6. As mentioned previously, throughout the session are study aids that provide background information on the passage, insights from commentaries, and word studies. Reading these aloud during the meeting is optional and up to the discussion leader. However, each member can refer to these insights if they found them helpful in understanding the passage.

A Note on Topical Studies

LifeChange guides offer a robust and thoughtful engagement with God's Word. The book-centric guides focus on a step-by-step walk through that particular book of the Bible. The topical studies use Scripture to help you engage more deeply with God's Word and its implications for your life.

INTRODUCTION

Forgiveness

WHY DO WE FORGIVE?

Forgiveness means releasing those who have wronged us from the relational debt they have created. But the very idea runs counter to what we think should happen when someone causes harm. When a victim's family extends forgiveness to a violent criminal, such after the 2015 Emanuel AME Church shooting in Charleston, South Carolina, we wonder whether forgiving means compromising justice or delaying healthy grief.[1] When we see those in genocide-ravaged Rwanda choosing to lay aside hatred and work toward not only forgiveness but also reconciliation, we wonder if that kind of restoration is even possible.[2]

And yet, something in us knows that forgiveness makes room for healing and restoration and helps us exchange spiritual turmoil for peace. Even medical science shows us this: Practicing forgiveness, even after deeply traumatic events, helps protect the cardiovascular system, improves mental health, and extends life expectancy.[3]

Forgiveness is both counterintuitive and compelling. First-century audiences must have also wrestled with this reality when Jesus talked about forgiveness in His Sermon on the Mount: the revolutionary call to love and pray for enemies (Matthew 5:44) and to forgive others (Matthew 6:14). The apostle Paul also challenged the family of the Lord Jesus Christ to be characterized by a posture of forgiveness: "Bear with each other and forgive one another if any of you has a grievance against someone. Forgive as the Lord forgave you" (Colossians 3:13).

So why do we forgive? Paul's answer emphasizes a form of the term *forgive* three times in a scant few words. We forgive because Jesus Himself exemplified such a posture, forgiving humanity's debt of sin through His sacrificial death on the cross.

To be identified with Christ, then, is to look and act increasingly like Him through the transforming work of the Holy Spirit, right down to His forgiving nature. Scripture shows us that forgiveness is an integral part of God's character. In this LifeChange guide, we will trace the concept of forgiveness across both the Old and New Testaments to discover more about the God who forgives and examine how He empowers us to forgive others.

FORGIVENESS IN THE KINGDOM OF GOD

Matthew 6:5-15

IN 1947, CORRIE TEN BOOM, a Dutch Christian who had been interned in Germany's Ravensbrück concentration camp for hiding Jews from the Nazis, reentered the country where she had been brutally treated and her dear sister died. Her reason? To tell Germans gathered at a Munich church about the God who forgives. "When we confess our sins," she declared, "God casts them into the deepest ocean, gone forever."

As she prepared to leave the church, she recognized a face in the room: "I saw him, working his way forward against the others. One moment I saw the overcoat and the brown hat; the next, a blue uniform and a visored cap with its skull and crossbones."

The man was her former guard from the concentration camp. "I have become a Christian," he said. "I know that God has forgiven me for the cruel things I did there, but I would like to hear it from your lips as well. *Fräulein*, will you forgive me?"

Corrie recounted, "I wrestled with the most difficult thing I had ever had to do. For I had to do it—I knew that. The message that God forgives has a prior condition: that we forgive those who have injured us. 'If you do not forgive men their trespasses,' Jesus says, 'neither will your Father in heaven forgive your trespasses.'"

Corrie realized in that moment that she could call on Jesus to help her forgive: to make a choice, a decision to follow the One who called her rather than to respond out of emotion. She took the man's outstretched hand, and as she later recounted, "This healing warmth seemed to flood my whole being, bringing tears to my eyes." She was able to forgive him with her whole heart.[1]

Corrie's dilemma is ours: We may believe in theory that we should forgive others when they sin against us, but the gulf between theory and application widens as we feel the weight of the harm. But as Corrie noted, Jesus' teaching on forgiveness in the Sermon on the Mount (Matthew 5–7) does not seem to offer exceptions. Instead, His teaching points to a way forward in our dilemma— the "how" of forgiveness—while also orienting us to ask why forgiveness matters so much in God's Kingdom.

---

1. Read Matthew 6:5-15. Verses 9-13 are perhaps the most often quoted prayer of all time. What details stand out to you as you read the Lord's Prayer within the larger context of the passage?

_____

_____

_____

_____

_____

_____

_____

New Testament scholar Craig S. Keener explains: "Having summarized Jesus' message as repentance in view of the coming kingdom (4:17), Matthew now collects Jesus' teachings that explain how a repentant person ready for God's rule should live. Only those submitted to God's reign now [in their present lives] are truly prepared for the time when he will judge the world and reign there unchallenged. This sermon provides examples of the self-sacrificial ethics of the kingdom, which its citizens must learn to exemplify even in the present world before the rest of the world recognizes that kingdom (6:10)."[2]

2. What contrasts do you notice between the model prayer (Matthew 6:9-13) and the prayers described in Matthew 6:5-8? What do these contrasts reveal about the relationship between the ones praying and God?

_____

_____

_____

_____

_____

_____

_____

3. Bible scholar Michael J. Wilkins notes that the structure of the model prayer moves from the worship and prioritization of the Father (Matthew 6:9-10) to a focus "on the needs of the individual disciples—their sustenance, their sin, and their spiritual battle" in verses 11-13.[3] How does verse 12 address the problem of a disciple's sin?

_____

_____

_____

_____

_____

_____

_____

_____

_____

_____

_____

4. Read another instance of Jesus' model prayer in Luke 11:1-4. What additional insights do you gain from Luke's wording in 11:4?

_____

_____

_____

_____

_____

_____

_____

_____

_____

5. In Matthew 6:14-15, what do you discover about the relationship between forgiving others and being forgiven by God? How might this relate to the larger discussion of hypocritical or pagan prayers in Matthew 6:5-7?

_____

_____

_____

_____

_____

_____

Michael J. Wilkins suggests, "[Matthew 6] does not teach that humans must forgive others before they can receive forgiveness themselves; rather, forgiveness of others is *proof* that that disciple's sins are forgiven and he or she possesses salvation (cf. 18:21-35). Disciples are to forgive those who have wronged them to maintain a joyful experience of our salvation (cf. 6:14-15). Doing so serves as evidence that a person has truly been forgiven his or her debt of sin. If we don't forgive, it is evidence that we haven't experienced forgiveness ourselves. . . . Salvation does not rest on human merits but only on the grace and mercy of God. Once disciples have received forgiveness and salvation, they are to forgive with the same forgiveness with which they have been forgiven."[4]

6. In Jesus' day, people viewed the religious elite (the Pharisees and the teachers of the law) as the epitome of righteousness because of how strictly they kept the religious laws and traditions. However, one of the themes of Jesus' Sermon on the Mount (Matthew 5-7) is that entering the Kingdom of Heaven requires a righteousness that "surpasses that of the Pharisees and the teachers of the law" (Matthew 5:20). How might Jesus' warning about withholding forgiveness prompt His listeners to look beyond themselves for the power and righteousness to be forgiven and to forgive?

_____

_____

_____

_____

_____

_____

7. Considering what Jesus taught about prayer
   (Matthew 6:5-7) and how disciples are to live as
   citizens of God's Kingdom (Matthew 5-7), what
   should be our attitude as we seek forgiveness for
   ourselves? Our attitude and posture as we seek to
   forgive others?

   _____

   _____

   _____

   _____

   _____

   _____

   _____

   _____

   _____

   _____

8. Jesus included forgiveness for self and others as
   part of petitioning or asking God for daily needs.
   How does this reorient us to ask God for help with
   forgiveness?

   _____

   _____

   _____

   _____

   _____

   _____

   _____

   _____

   _____

9. Consider a time when you had difficulty feeling that you were forgiven by God. What obstacles made it difficult to approach God or accept God's gift of forgiving your debts? How might you use the Lord's Prayer as a model to ask the Father for help in receiving forgiveness?

_____

_____

_____

_____

_____

_____

_____

_____

_____

10. Now consider a time when you had difficulty forgiving another person. What obstacles made it difficult to forgive your debtors? How might you use the Lord's Prayer as a model to ask the Father for help in forgiving others?

_____

_____

_____

_____

_____

_____

_____

_____

_____

11. Pastor and Greek scholar Eugene Peterson offered a modern paraphrase of Matthew 6:12 as "keep us forgiven with you and forgiving others" (MSG). How might our relationships and communities look different if Christ followers, the citizens of God's Kingdom, regularly asked for God's help to live this way?

Your Response

Following His teaching of the model prayer as recorded in Luke's Gospel (Luke 11:1-4), Jesus expanded on the idea that when we pray, God hears and answers (Luke 11:5-13). Jesus encouraged His listeners to "ask and it will be given to you; seek and you will find; knock and the door will be opened to you" (Luke 11:9). What questions about forgiveness are you asking God to answer during this study? What aspects of forgiveness are you seeking to explore and understand more fully?

_____

_____

_____

_____

_____

_____

_____

_____

_____

_____

_____

_____

_____

_____

_____

_____

_____

_____

_____

For Further Study

Read Ephesians 4:25-32. How might unforgiveness affect the body of Christ? How might it grieve the Holy Spirit? What did Paul suggest is the better way forward (Ephesians 4:31-32)?

Session Two

THE GOD WHO FORGIVES

Exodus 34:1-10

NO DOUBT IT STARTED AS A WHISPER, a murmur of skepticism, fear, or impatience that began to spread from one person to the next. Soon, though, that first rumor had grown into the roar of certainty: "This fellow Moses who brought us up out of Egypt" was not coming back down Mount Sinai (Exodus 32:1). Surely it must be time to take charge and make a new plan.

For forty days and nights, Moses had been with God on a mountain in the wilderness, learning God's provisions and instructions for the nation He had freed and chosen as His own. God had even carved the Ten Commandments with His own finger to outline His covenant with His people (Exodus 31:18). Yet, while waiting down in the camp, the newly freed nation of Israel entertained doubt. Where was Moses? Why was he taking so long?

That doubt opened the door to sin. The people surrounded Aaron to declare, "Come, make us gods who will go before us. As for this fellow Moses who brought us up out of Egypt, we don't know what has happened to him" (Exodus 32:1). Aaron complied, making a golden calf from the people's donated jewelry, and "the next day the people rose early and sacrificed burnt offerings and presented fellowship offerings. Afterward they sat down to eat and drink and got up to indulge in revelry" (Exodus 32:6).

Upon witnessing their sin, Moses smashed the first set of stone tablets, a graphic depiction of Israel's broken faith with their God. Mere weeks after experiencing God's deliverance from Egypt and declaring, "We will do everything the LORD has said" (Exodus 19:8), God's chosen people were partying around an idol.

We may shake our heads in wonder, and yet how often do we find ourselves doing the same? Our idols are different, but we, too, can find ourselves clinging

11

to areas of sin—actions, motivations, and distractions—that keep us distant from the One who rescued us, wondering how we find our way back to Him.

Exodus shows us the path. Against the backdrop of Israel's blatant disobedience, God meets with Moses a second time to illuminate how we humans, despite the corrupting force of sin at work in us, can hope to have a relationship with a holy and righteous God.

1. Read Exodus 34:1-10. Note a few of the details of the circumstances and setting that particularly catch your attention. Why do those things stand out to you?

_____

_____

_____

_____

_____

_____

_____

"Before He did anything with the tablets," wrote Bible teacher Warren Wiersbe, "God proclaimed the greatness of His attributes (Ex. 34:5-7), a declaration that is basic to all Jewish and Christian theology. Moses repeated these words to God at Kadesh-Barnea (Num. 14:17-19), the Jews used them in Nehemiah's day (Neh. 9:17-18), and Jonah quoted them when he sat pouting outside Nineveh (Jonah 4:1-2)."[1]

2. In verses 5-7, God proclaimed His covenant name (Yahweh or "I AM," denoted as LORD in most English translations) before declaring some of the realities of His character. The whole of Exodus 34:1-10 contains both explicit and implied character qualities or attributes of God. Which attributes of God do you observe in these ten verses?

_____

_____

_____

_____

_____

_____

3. Exodus 33:18-23 records God's opening inter-
action with Moses ahead of this encounter. What
did God say would happen if Moses were to see
His "face" or full glory?

_____

_____

_____

_____

_____

_____

_____

_____

_____

_____

4. What protective measures did God provide
(Exodus 33:21-23)? What other protections did
God prescribe in Exodus 34:3?

_____

_____

_____

_____

_____

_____

_____

_____

_____

_____

_____

_____

"This is the most elevated glimpse of God Moses has ever had and will have. This is not the burning bush [Exodus 3], which prompted Moses' curiosity to take a closer look. . . . Their relationship has deepened, and so, too, the degree to which God reveals himself to Moses. So, unlike the relatively 'tame' theophany [an appearance of God] of chapter 3, Moses now catches a glimpse of God that, if God were to remove his hand, would bring death even to him."[2]

5. What attributes of God do these protective measures reveal?

_____

_____

_____

_____

_____

_____

_____

_____

_____

_____

_____

6. From the outworking of His character (who God *is*) flow God's actions (what God *does*). What actions did God specifically proclaim in Exodus 34:7? Why might any of these seem surprising?

_____

_____

_____

_____

_____

_____

_____

_____

_____

_____

7. In Exodus 34:7, what kinds of things did God say He forgives?

_____

_____

_____

_____

_____

_____

_____

_____

_____

_____

_____

_____

8. Why would this wide range of forgivable offenses be encouraging in light of Israel's behavior in Exodus 32?

_____

_____

_____

_____

_____

_____

_____

_____

_____

_____

_____

_____

God proclaims Himself as One who forgives *avon* (a Hebrew term "meaning iniquity, evil, guilt"),[3] *pesha* ("transgression, rebellion"),[4] and *chatta'ah* ("sin, transgression"),[5] leaving no doubt of His power and authority to forgive sin, whether innate wickedness, intentional rebellion, or actions that miss the mark of righteousness in any other way.

"As in the ten commandments (20:5-6), this expression [in Exodus 34:7] shows that the iniquity and its punishment will continue in the family if left unchecked. This does not go on as long as the outcomes for good (thousands versus third or fourth generations), and it is limited to those who hate God."[6]

9. Compare the remainder of Exodus 34:7 ("Yet he does not leave the guilty unpunished; he punishes the children and their children for the sin of the parents to the third and fourth generation") with an earlier version of this same statement in Exodus 20:4-6. What do these passages suggest about the consequences of sin—especially replacing worship of God with idol worship—when that sin is not addressed through repentance and forgiveness?

_____

_____

_____

_____

_____

_____

_____

The science of epigenetics examines "tiny chemical tags [that] are added to or removed from our DNA in response to changes in the environment in which we are living . . . turn[ing] genes on or off" to adapt. This genetic metadata allows information to pass from one generation to the next at the biological level. Though the genetic code itself is not mutated, the "tags" from traumatic events a person experiences may impact the health and well-being of future children by changing how their genes react to their own environment.[7]

10. Though Christians are not under the old covenant between God and the nation of Israel, we often see God's larger principles at work. What evidence have you seen of generational consequences for unaddressed sin or generational blessing out of forgiveness and restoration? Why do you think this may be?

_____

_____

_____

_____

_____

_____

_____

_____

11. After what one scholar calls Moses' "elevated glimpse of God," how did Moses respond (Exodus 34:8-9)? Describe a time when you got a clearer glimpse of who God is and what He does. How did you respond?

_____

_____

_____

_____

_____

_____

_____

_____

_____

12. How does Exodus 34:10 show that God answered Moses' prayer for forgiveness? What are ways you have experienced God's forgiveness in your own life?

_____

_____

_____

_____

_____

_____

_____

_____

_____

Your Response

From the very inception of God's covenant with
Israel, His people showed themselves incapable
of keeping His law. Indeed, throughout the Bible
and history we find humans falling short because
of sin, which entered and corrupted human
nature when the first humans disobeyed God.
However, through it all God revealed something
far more powerful than the rebellious nature of
humans: *His* nature, including His compassion,
graciousness, patience, love, faithfulness,
forgiveness, and justice. Which of these attributes
of God are you prompted to thank Him for this
week? Are there any areas of sin that you need to
acknowledge to Him and ask Him to forgive?

For Further Study

In Exodus 34:8-9, we observe Moses interceding for the people of Israel. This is one of many times he would function in this role (see Exodus 32:30-35 and 33:12-17). Moses also foreshadowed Jesus Christ as an intercessor.

Read 1 John 2:1-2. How is Jesus described here? What was Jesus able to accomplish that Moses could not? How does the nature of Christ as righteous advocate and atoning sacrifice encourage you in any area where you struggle with sin? How could you encourage someone else with this good news?

FORESHADOWING FORGIVENESS

Leviticus 16:1-20

NINETEEN-YEAR-OLD POOJA was volunteering at a local hospital, preparing to study psychology at her university, when she began learning about Jesus from a fellow volunteer. A devout Hindu, Pooja had been faithful to practice her religion's rituals—offerings at the altar in her home, fasting, and meditation—hoping they would bring her closer to what she worshiped. She loved the elements of her religion but always sensed something missing. Did Jesus and Christianity hold answers?

The concept of sin, though, felt foreign to Pooja:

> I thought, *How am I a sinner?* I've been a good person all my life and tried to stay one step ahead through my religion. But I realized that I always had a restless urge to try to be good enough for long enough. My rituals (like not eating certain foods, or doing meditations) would help for a while, but then the feeling that I was good enough would go away. I longed to help people through therapy, but I could not ignore how my own thoughts—like jealousy and envy, or my sadness and desperation to make things right when I hurt others—pointed to something broken inside me. How could I help others as a counselor if I couldn't explain what was going on with myself? That's when I realized that sin was not just about actions but about even my thoughts and feelings. I needed Jesus' saving grace and forgiveness and His Holy Spirit to guide me.[1]

Pooja recognized an underlying issue in her soul that she could not overcome through her religious practice.

Even when her rituals led to a peaceful feeling, that peace was only temporary. Without realizing it, she was noticing the separation between her and God because something was broken at a fundamental level. Pooja longed for reconciliation and lasting peace with God.

In the Old Testament God set up a system of sacrifices to atone for the sin and brokenness of His people so that He could have a relationship with them. The somber Day of Atonement marked the moment each year when the people of Israel would know that "before the LORD, you will be clean from all your sins" (Leviticus 16:30). Then the people would enter a new year of sins and subsequent sacrifices that would allow Israel to have a relationship with God. Unlike the rituals of other religions, however, this system pointed forward to a time when it would no longer be needed: when God in the flesh, Jesus, would offer His own life of sinless perfection, rather than unblemished lambs or bulls, as a final sacrifice to provide a permanent means of forgiveness and reconciliation.

The Hebrew term *kāpar*, from which the Day of Atonement or Yom Kippur gets its name, is one of the Hebrew terms associated with forgiveness in the Old Testament and is often translated "to atone, wipe clean, appease."[2] William Mounce notes, "As described in Lev. 16 (*kāpar* occurs 16x), the Day of Atonement was a day of purging sins from the holy sanctuary. All throughout the year, the priest sprinkled the blood of sacrificial animals in front of the curtain of the sanctuary (e.g., 4:6) and thus symbolically transferred the sins of God's people into his Holy Place. By the end of the year, that place was, as it were, filled up with all their sins. Something had to be done in order to 'clean house'; this was the purpose of the Day of Atonement. Note how in the final stage of the ceremony, the sins of God's people were placed on the head of the live goat, who then carried them far away into the desert, never to be seen again. There was now 'room' for another year's worth of sin in the Most Holy Place."[3]

1. Read Leviticus 16:1-20. Which details stand out or seem surprising to you? Why do you think these details catch your attention?

_____

_____

_____

_____

_____

_____

_____

_____

_____

_____

_____

2. Who were all the individuals or groups of people involved in observing Yom Kippur, the Day of Atonement? What were some specific ways they had to prepare?

_____

_____

_____

_____

_____

_____

_____

_____

_____

_____

_____

3. How many and what kinds of sacrifices do you notice in the passage?

_____

_____

_____

_____

_____

_____

_____

_____

_____

_____

_____

"[Sin] is dreadful for our well-being, divisive in our relationships, destructive to the environment. Sin deceives, entices, and enslaves. Sin perverts our physical being, psychological health, and spiritual make-up. Sin brings conflict, culpability, contamination, and corruption. Sin is positively fatal for our relationship with God. Indeed, sin is our enemy (1 Cor 15:26)."[4]

4. Consider the sheer number and intricacy of details described in this passage. What might those indicate about the seriousness of sin and its effect on the relationship between God and humans?

_____

_____

_____

_____

_____

_____

_____

_____

_____

_____

5. Read Hebrews 10:1-4. How does the writer characterize the sacrificial system put in place by Old Testament law?

_____

_____

_____

_____

_____

_____

_____

_____

_____

_____

_____

6. Why was the sacrificial system a temporary solution to the problem of sin?

_____

_____

_____

_____

_____

_____

_____

_____

_____

_____

7. Read Hebrews 10:5-10. How did Jesus end the need for the sacrificial system and provide a permanent means of forgiveness for sin?

_____

_____

_____

_____

_____

_____

_____

_____

_____

_____

_____

N. T. Wright offers this perspective: "The regular round of sacrifices under the old covenant could never address the problem of sin and guilt in the *consciences* of the worshippers (verse 2). They could, after their own fashion, effect purification from outward impurities. . . . They could never achieve the deep cleansing, the healing of memories and imaginations, that the blood of Jesus has achieved and can achieve. They couldn't, in that sense, 'take sins away,' restoring sinful human beings to an actual condition in which their consciences had been rinsed clean, enabling them to stand boldly and gladly in the presence of God."[5]

8. For those "made holy" by trusting in Christ's sacrifice (Hebrews 10:10), how might this permanent means of forgiveness also allow for a deeper relationship with God than what those under the Old Testament sacrificial system would have been able to experience?

_____

_____

_____

_____

_____

_____

_____

_____

_____

9. With forgiveness assured through accepting Christ's "once for all" sacrifice (Hebrews 10:10), why do you think we still practice historic Christian disciplines such as prayer, fasting, reading Scripture, and worship? Do they earn us God's acceptance and forgiveness? Why or why not?

_____

_____

_____

_____

_____

_____

_____

_____

10. What have you experienced or noticed when you trust in your own actions as a means of making things right with God? What is different when you depend instead on Christ's actions on our behalf?

_____

_____

_____

_____

_____

_____

_____

_____

_____

_____

11. How might understanding the role of the Old Testament sacrificial system as the foreshadowing of Christ's solution for sin help you trust Christ's sacrifice more thoroughly? How might this perspective help you encourage others who are seeking forgiveness and acceptance from God?

_____

_____

_____

_____

_____

_____

_____

_____

_____

Your Response

Sin is serious because it separates people from God—which is why Christ's sacrifice to provide forgiveness for sin was immense, mending that vast separation forever. As you reflect on this reality, in what ways do the passages from Leviticus and Hebrews hit home for you? Are there any areas of your life where you believe God cannot forgive you? Do you find yourself continually attempting to do enough "good" things to make up for those areas? How might you ask God to help you better understand that Jesus is the way to forgiveness and acceptance in every part of life?

_____

_____

_____

_____

_____

_____

_____

_____

_____

_____

_____

_____

_____

_____

_____

_____

_____

_____

For Further Study

Read Romans 7:21–8:13. How does Paul emphasize the human dilemma of sin and the solution Jesus Christ offers? Why are those who trust in Christ's sacrifice free from condemnation? How do they experience freedom from the enslavement of sin even though they still deal with occasional sinful thoughts or actions? In what ways do Christians "put to death the misdeeds of the body" (Romans 8:13) and thus experience abundant life?

THE GOSPEL OF FORGIVENESS

Luke 23:32-43

MASON WAS A GIFTED, goal-oriented student, confident he could achieve "the good life" through thinking rationally and working hard. That meant he had little time for God or Christianity. In fact, he says, he quietly mocked his Christian classmates for their "blind faith," particularly those whose behavior seemed the same or even worse than his. According to Mason,

> Life was essentially a meritocracy—your value was based on your abilities, talents, and accomplishments. My identity and self-worth were rooted in academic and musical pursuits. However, that self-reliance started to unravel as I continued to face something I couldn't overcome with natural abilities or sheer grit and determination. Specifically, I was addicted to pornography, which had begun when I was around twelve and continued year after year.
>
> Even though I didn't care what God or the Bible had to say, there was something within me that told me that it was wrong. Whenever the high would wear off from looking at porn, I was overwhelmed with feeling dirty and ashamed, unable to break the cycle. Each failure led to more guilt, shame, and depression, all of which I kept hidden. But a faithful friend began to engage me in spiritual conversations and invite me to a college Bible study. I wasn't overly impressed at first, but I kept going until one night, the Lord started opening my eyes to

Him and His good news. I can still remember the leader standing in the middle of the room, saying, "There is nothing you can do to make God love you more and nothing you can do to make God love you less." That truth hit me, and I felt the weight lift from having to earn love, approval, and self-worth through my actions. I could hardly believe that because of Jesus, God was willing to forgive me for the things for which I couldn't even forgive myself, but after several weeks I came to trust that Jesus was who He said He was, that He really lived a perfect life, really died on the cross for my sins, and really resurrected from the grave. I was overwhelmed with His love and convinced that by trusting Him as my Lord and Savior, I could be forgiven.[1]

Today, Mason, the former skeptic, is a pastor who uses his own story to connect with those skeptical about Christianity, helping them see the truth and grace found in Jesus Christ.

The Gospel writer Luke also understood the power of people's life-changing encounters with Jesus, and he shared stories that illuminate who Christ was and the good news of forgiveness and rescue through His death and resurrection (see Luke 1:1-4). Even in the midst of Jesus' crucifixion, observers witnessed Him demonstrating that He was the sinless sacrifice for humanity's rebellion. They recounted hearing Him say that He was the source of forgiveness and eternal life. For one doomed criminal on a cross next to Jesus, that truth would turn the worst day of his life into an eternal future of life with God as he became "the first of many [to have] positive responses to the cross."[2]

1. Read Luke 23:32-43. What details stand out to you or seem surprising?

_____

_____

_____

_____

_____

_____

_____

_____

_____

_____

2. Who are the various people or groups in this scene? What are they doing and saying?

_____

_____

_____

_____

_____

_____

_____

_____

_____

_____

_____

The high traffic near the Crucifixion and the number of people interacting would not have been unusual for a Roman execution. Roman accounts from the time state: "Whenever we crucify the guilty, the most crowded roads are chosen, where the most people can see and be moved by this fear."[3] New Testament scholar Darrell Bock comments that Luke makes use of this "variety of observers" to tell the story, and that "as has been his custom, we see the Passion through many eyes and in varying perspectives."[4]

3. Do any of the actions or words you notice contrast with each other or seem ironic against the backdrop of the Crucifixion? If so, how?

4. Consider Jesus' prayer in Luke 23:34: "Father, forgive them, for they do not know what they are doing." Bible scholar David Crowther admits, "It is difficult to know who all 'them' includes."[5] For whom might Jesus have been interceding to ask that the Father forgive and for what reason(s)?

5. Read Jesus' teaching in Luke 6:27-36 and compare it with His intercessory prayer on the cross (Luke 23:34). By asking for God's mercy for others, how was Jesus living out that teaching from His humanity (Jesus as fully human acting toward humans)?

_____

_____

_____

_____

_____

_____

_____

_____

6. How was Jesus living out that teaching from His divinity (Jesus as fully God acting toward humans)? Why might those crucifying Him need immediate forgiveness and mercy?

_____

_____

_____

_____

_____

_____

_____

_____

_____

_____

7. Luke 23:35-39 focuses on Jesus' identity as "king," "God's . . . Chosen One," and "Messiah" (a word meaning "anointed," which is also the meaning of the term *christos*, the Greek word from which we get *Christ*). Which words does Luke use to describe the tone and attitudes of the various people using these terms?

_____

_____

_____

_____

_____

_____

_____

_____

_____

_____

"It was providential that Jesus was crucified *between* the two thieves, for this gave both of them equal access to the Saviour. Both could read Pilate's superscription, 'This is Jesus of Nazareth the King of the Jews,' and both could watch Him as He graciously gave His life for the sins of the world.

"The one thief imitated the mockery of the religious leaders and asked Jesus to rescue him from the cross, but the other thief had different ideas. He may have reasoned, 'If this Man is indeed the Christ, and if He has a kingdom, and if He has saved others, then He can meet my greatest need which is salvation from sin. I am not ready to die!'"[6]

8. In what ways did the second criminal (Luke 23:40-42) display a tone and an attitude that sharply contrasted with those of the other speakers? Though the text does not say *why* he reacted in this way, what could be some possible reasons?

_____

_____

_____

_____

_____

_____

_____

_____

9. How did the second criminal characterize his own actions and the consequences of those actions in Luke 23:40-41? What did he proclaim about Jesus?

_____

_____

_____

_____

_____

_____

_____

_____

_____

_____

_____

10. Jesus and the criminals were approaching certain death. Yet the second criminal made a striking request: "Jesus, remember me when you come into your kingdom" (Luke 23:42). What does this request demonstrate about the man's faith?

_____

_____

_____

_____

_____

_____

_____

_____

_____

"Theologically, the cross provides the atonement that forgives sin. Jesus offers himself here in service to others. He prays for the forgiveness of his enemies and accepts one of the criminals into his kingdom. He represents us as he unjustly bears the penalty for our sin in his love. The most important consideration we can give to the cross is to embrace its meaning with a responsive heart that is filled with the forgiveness, love, and humility Jesus so eloquently displays here. The only action that does the cross of Christ justice is to welcome its work with an all-embracing faith."[7]

11. Have you ever observed or experienced unexpected faith in God in the midst of dire circumstances? What was the result?

_____

_____

_____

_____

_____

_____

_____

_____

_____

_____

12. Ephesians 1:7-8 says, "In [Christ] we have redemption through his blood, the forgiveness of sins, in accordance with the riches of God's grace that he lavished on us." How did Jesus' response to the criminal (Luke 23:43) reveal this principle?

_____

_____

_____

_____

_____

_____

_____

_____

_____

_____

13. In response to the second criminal's simplistic confession and appeal, Jesus promised, "Today you will be with me in paradise." Why might it be difficult to accept that promise? Why might the dying criminal's words and Jesus' response be encouraging?

_____

_____

_____

_____

_____

_____

_____

_____

_____

_____

_____

_____

_____

_____

_____

_____

_____

_____

_____

_____

_____

_____

_____

_____

Your Response

The second criminal trusted in Jesus just before his own death with no opportunity to live a reformed life and no chance to make amends for wrongs done. How do you respond to this reality? Do you find it challenging? Encouraging?

Now consider the gospel (literally, "good news") of Jesus Christ: that He lived the sinless life we could not live, that He willingly died the death we deserved for our sins, that He rose again from the grave, conquering sin and death, and that He offers forgiveness and eternal life to all who entrust themselves to Him. What, if any, parts of the gospel are difficult to understand or accept fully? Whom might you talk to about those areas this week?

For Further Study

Under the inspiration of the Holy Spirit, the New Testament writers pointed to the many ways in which Jesus fulfilled Old Testament prophecies during His earthly ministry. Even His crucifixion alongside criminals was a fulfillment of Isaiah 53:12, as Jesus Himself explained in Luke 22:37. Read all of Isaiah 53. What stands out to you about the description of the Suffering Servant of God who would "[bear] the sin of many, and [make] intercession for the transgressors" (Isaiah 53:12)?

_____

_____

_____

_____

_____

_____

_____

_____

_____

_____

_____

_____

_____

_____

_____

_____

_____

_____

_____

REPENTING AND RECEIVING FORGIVENESS

Psalm 51

SPRINGTIME WAS WHEN ancient kings traditionally pushed forward in battle. But one year, Israel's warrior champion, their giant slayer, decided to stay home. Why King David sent his armies out to war without joining them is unclear, but that decision marked a season of turning from God and plunging into sin with destructive consequences.

Second Samuel 11–12 details how David committed adultery, coveting the wife of one of his soldiers and using his power and privilege to secure what he wanted. He then staged a cover-up of her pregnancy, eventually ordering her husband moved to the front lines to be killed in battle. Though this enabled David to marry Bathsheba and obscure his dishonorable conduct (a move that some scholars say would have been acceptable in the honor/shame-based cultures of ancient Israel and surrounding kingdoms since it preserved the surface reputations of all involved[1]), 2 Samuel 11:27 says that "the thing David had done displeased the LORD." God used the prophet Nathan to rebuke David and force him to face his actions.

Psalm 51 reflects David's response to the rebuke: As he confronts his own depravity and the weight of his sin, he cries out to God for mercy and forgiveness. Though the natural consequences of his actions played out for decades through tragedies and betrayals within his family, David did receive forgiveness from God (2 Samuel 12:13).

The final two verses of the psalm widen the lens to encompass national Israel, which some scholars believe indicates how David's words came to be used as a model to "[make] David's penitence their own, adding these verses to make their prayer specific."[2] So it can be for us. David's words of brokenhearted humility as he casts himself fully on God's mercy can guide us along the path to receive forgiveness.

1. Read Psalm 51. Which words or phrases resonate with you?

_____

_____

_____

_____

_____

_____

_____

_____

_____

Psalm 51 shares commonalities with six other psalms (6, 32, 38, 102, 130, and 143) that petition God for mercy and forgiveness. Scholars identify these as the penitential psalms.

Old Testament scholar Tremper Longman III writes, "The psalmist grounds the appeal [for forgiveness] not in anything that he has done, but rather in the character of God, who exhibits *unfailing love* (ḥesed, a word that could also be translated 'loyalty') and *great compassion*. Both of these characteristics are grounded in the covenant that God made with Israel and are cited in God's great statement of self-definition found in Exodus 34:6 and elsewhere."[3]

2. Do any words or phrases remind you of other Bible passages? (See the callout for ideas.) What do you notice as you compare and contrast those?

_____

_____

_____

_____

_____

_____

_____

_____

_____

_____

3. In Psalm 51:1-14, what are some of the terms David uses for the concept of sin or being in a sinful state? If you have access to other translations, what are some additional terms you observe in these verses?

_____

_____

_____

_____

_____

_____

_____

_____

_____

_____

4. Just as David uses multiple words to paint a fuller picture of sin, he also employs multiple images for the forgiveness he's seeking from God. In verses 1-14, what are the different actions David pleads for God to take in order to remove sin from him?

_____

_____

_____

_____

_____

_____

_____

_____

_____

_____

The 2 Samuel context for Psalm 51 clearly indicates David's sin harmed multiple people, and yet, the psalmist states: "Against you, you only, have I sinned" (Psalm 51:4). This may be rhetorical overstatement to underscore, as the New English Translation renders the Hebrew phrasing, "Against you—you above all—I have sinned." Longman suggests: "Perhaps this statement is to be taken as a hyperbolic recognition that, as horrible as the consequences are to human beings, the most egregious part of sin is the rebellion against God. Again, the psalm, although inspired by the David and Bathsheba event, is not restricted to that event, since it is written for community use, but the principle still stands for all sins. Sin typically has ramifications for the people around us, but the psalmist reminds us that, as bad as that is, the worse offence is against God."[4]

5. Taken together, what might these multiple images of sin and forgiveness suggest about the seriousness of sin and its effect on the relationship between humans and God?

6. Review Psalm 51:5, 10-12. How do these verses highlight a larger problem beyond individual sins? What does David long for beyond forgiveness for a particular sin?

7. As detailed in Leviticus, God provided an extensive system of sacrifices (many of them done daily) to atone for sin. He even required a solemn day of fasting and special sacrifices each year to cleanse the accumulated sins of the people (Leviticus 16). What do David's words in Psalm 51:16-17 suggest about the Old Testament sacrificial system as a solution for sin? What does God long for beyond outward sacrifices (Psalm 51:17)?

_____

_____

_____

_____

_____

_____

_____

_____

8. What does Hebrews 10:11-14 in the New Testament say that Christ, functioning as both high priest and sacrifice, accomplished through His death and resurrection? How do those verses encourage a Christ follower regarding God's response to a "broken and contrite heart" (Psalm 51:17)?

_____

_____

_____

_____

_____

_____

_____

_____

_____

Derek Kidner outlines David's progression from desperate plea for mercy to confession to restored confidence that God will cleanse him to inward renewal. "The depth of self-knowledge seen in verses 3-5 might have led to despair," but instead that knowledge increases David's prayers for a changed heart. Kidner notes that by verse 15, where David pleads for the Lord to open his lips so he may declare praise, David moves from a "conscience [that] has shamed him into silence" to a "heartfelt, humble plea [that] leads the worshipper in one step from confession to the brink of praise."[5]

9. What does Psalm 51:13-19 suggest can result from an individual being forgiven, cleansed, and restored to the joy of salvation?

_____

_____

_____

_____

_____

_____

_____

_____

_____

_____

10. Have you witnessed joy being restored through repentance and forgiveness, whether in your own life or in others'? What did that look or feel like?

_____

_____

_____

_____

_____

_____

_____

_____

_____

_____

11. Those who have been forgiven and restored are able to point to God's goodness or encourage others in their struggles. In what ways might forgiveness and restoration have a ripple effect in a family or community?

_____

_____

_____

_____

_____

_____

_____

_____

_____

_____

_____

_____

_____

_____

_____

_____

_____

_____

_____

_____

_____

_____

Your Response

David's psalm demonstrates honest repentance and confession, dependence on God's merciful forgiveness and cleansing, and an anticipation of overflowing joy in forgiveness. As you spend time in prayer this week, ask God to illuminate any sins for which you need forgiveness. Are there any thoughts, actions, or areas of struggle that you would like to confess to Him? How might you turn to Him with "a broken and contrite [remorseful] heart" (Psalm 51:17)? Remember that God is merciful, loving, and compassionate (Psalm 51:1) and that Jesus' sacrifice allows our sin nature to be dealt with once and for all. Ask God for forgiveness for any of the things that have come to mind, and thank Him for restoring the joy of His salvation (Psalm 51:12).

_____

_____

_____

_____

_____

_____

_____

_____

_____

_____

_____

_____

_____

_____

_____

For Further Study

Read Psalm 6, another penitential psalm, in which David asks God not only for gentleness in dealing with sin (Psalm 6:1) but also for mercy and help in great suffering and opposition. What do you learn about God's character in this psalm? What urgent requests does David make of God, and what expectation does he have that God will answer?

THE RESPONSE OF THE FORGIVEN

Luke 7:36-50

AS THE "SINGLES OVER THIRTY" class at Faithbridge Church in north Houston, Texas, started studying Jesus' parables, they reflected on how Jesus used story not only to illustrate spiritual truths but also to shake up His listeners and prompt them to respond, either with greater curiosity and faith or with doubt and rejection.

Parables are teachings from everyday life that illustrate truth. As the breakout-table discussion leaders reflected on how their own stories included Jesus' grace and restoration despite shattered dreams, loss and grief, divorce, gripping sin patterns, and seasons of doubt, they decided to add a twist to their study time. Every person in the group, they realized, could also tell their own kinds of parables, illustrating truth about Jesus and prompting others to respond to Him.

Each week, different leaders shared how Jesus shook them up and brought them to a place of freedom through radical dependence on Him. Without fail, even the most stoic of listeners shed a few tears at these testimonies—how God saw people in their places of need and moved toward them with mercy.

Perhaps the woman in today's passage would have felt right at home in that group. But such transparency and vulnerability might have sent another key figure in the passage—Simon the Pharisee—running in the opposite direction. At the very least, he would have been muttering under his breath at what he was hearing from others in the room. However, as Luke 7:36-50 demonstrates, Jesus had other ideas for Simon. Jesus combined a teaching parable with a real-life example of forgiveness to point Simon and His other listeners to truth.

1. Read Luke 7:36-50, focusing on the people and the setting. Where was Jesus, and what was He doing?

_____

_____

_____

_____

_____

_____

_____

_____

_____

_____

2. Scholars say such dinners took place in a room with open doors "so that interested people can enter, sit on the edge of the room, and hear the discussion" with noted public figures.[1] Who were the other people present at this dinner, and what details do you notice about them?

_____

_____

_____

_____

_____

_____

_____

_____

_____

_____

3. The "woman in that town who lived a sinful life" (Luke 7:37) took several actions, as described in Luke 7:37-38, 44-47. What did she do?

_____

_____

_____

_____

_____

_____

_____

_____

_____

_____

4. What did Simon the Pharisee say "to himself" in Luke 7:39? What do his thoughts indicate about his opinion of Jesus? Of the woman?

_____

_____

_____

_____

_____

_____

_____

_____

_____

_____

_____

Excavations of first-century (AD) sites in Israel have revealed the popularity of lachrymatories, or glass tear bottles, in Hellenistic culture. According to archaeologist Scott Stripling, it is possible that in addition to washing Jesus' feet with the tears falling from her eyes, the woman in this passage may have been emptying her tear bottle onto His feet before anointing them with costly perfume. The lachrymatory was where one saved tears as remembrances of the ups and downs of life, and often a woman would present those tears to her husband upon their marriage, symbolizing her trust in him and their new shared life. Stripling also notes that the loosening of the woman's hair to wipe Jesus' feet meant that her hair was now down in the style of a married woman, another powerful symbol of her total devotion to the One who had saved and forgiven her.[2]

5. Jesus was both teacher and prophet as He answered Simon's inner monologue with a short parable, inviting Simon to be the student and make some connections. But Jesus also pointed to greater truth about Himself. What does Jesus' story immediately following Simon's silent thought indicate about His prophetic powers? How does what Jesus said "answer" Simon?

_____

_____

_____

_____

_____

_____

_____

_____

_____

6. Reread Luke 7:41-43. How do the debts of five hundred denarii (almost two years' wages) and fifty denarii (almost two months' wages)[3] demonstrate principles about sin? (See also Matthew 6:12; Matthew 18:27; Colossians 2:14.)

_____

_____

_____

_____

_____

_____

_____

_____

_____

7. Who are the characters in the parable, and to whom or what might they correspond?

_____

_____

_____

_____

_____

_____

_____

_____

_____

_____

8. Jesus asked Simon in Luke 7:42, "Which of them will love him more?" How did Simon answer?

_____

_____

_____

_____

_____

_____

_____

_____

_____

_____

_____

David Crowther remarks: "The waywardness of the Pharisees and scribes is once again showcased in [Luke] 7:36-50. In this passage the focus is on recognizing one's need and indebtedness to God. First, a woman with a sullied reputation anoints Jesus' feet, and this provokes a critical response from the Pharisees. Jesus points out that she has done something wonderful for him and then tells a parable to show that those who are most humbly aware of their sinfulness demonstrate that awareness by feeling the greatest degree of grateful love."[4]

9. If Jesus had ended His teaching at the statement "You have judged correctly" (Luke 7:43), how might Simon have been tempted to interpret the parable in regards to himself and his life up to that point?

_____

_____

_____

_____

_____

_____

_____

_____

_____

10. In Luke 7:44-47, Jesus moved from parable to real life, comparing the weeping woman's actions with Simon's inactions. What, according to Jesus, did the woman's actions indicate about her heart? What did Simon's inactions indicate about his heart?

_____

_____

_____

_____

_____

_____

_____

_____

_____

_____

_____

11. The sinful woman was overwhelmed with love for God. Have you ever experienced an intense awareness of what God has done for you? How did you respond?

_____

_____

_____

_____

_____

_____

_____

_____

_____

12. How would Jesus' words to the woman in Luke 7:48, 50 have encouraged her? What did Jesus identify as a critical aspect of receiving forgiveness (Luke 7:50)?

_____

_____

_____

_____

_____

_____

_____

_____

_____

Darrell Bock points out that Jesus' "final comment is significant, since up to this point the issue has been the presence of love. Jesus' remark [about the woman's faith] reveals a crucial theological sequence: first an offer of forgiveness from God, then the faith that saves. Such faith evidences itself in the acts of love that she has performed for Jesus. Such is the fundamental cycle of relationship that exists between God and a believer."[5]

13. Consider a time when you were aware of your need for forgiveness. What was your approach to God? If you asked in faith to be forgiven, what emotions or shifts did you experience afterward?

_____

_____

_____

_____

_____

_____

_____

_____

14. How did the guests respond to the events of the dinner party (Luke 7:49)? By forgiving the woman's sin and sending her on her way in peace, what did Jesus reveal about Himself?

_____

_____

_____

_____

_____

_____

_____

_____

Your Response

In the verses that precede this dinner (Luke 7:1-35), the Gospel writer shows Jesus performing mighty miracles across the Judean countryside. Jesus made it clear that all His actions and words fulfilled Old Testament prophecy: that when the Messiah would come, "the blind receive sight, the lame walk, those who have leprosy are cleansed, the deaf hear, the dead are raised, and the good news is proclaimed to the poor" (Luke 7:22). On display at Simon's house was the good news that Jesus, God the Son, offers forgiveness to all who recognize their spiritual poverty and receive Him by faith.

How do you respond to this truth? Do you tend to respond more like Simon—relying on the externals of right living but not always aware that Jesus has "something to tell you" (Luke 7:40)? Or do you resonate more with the woman's response—overflowing with love for Jesus but not always confident that simple faith is enough to receive forgiveness for sin and peace with God? Talk to God this week about what keeps you from seeking or receiving His forgiveness.

For Further Study

About a week after Christ ascended into heaven,
the apostle Peter preached the gospel to a large
group of Jews gathered for the Pentecost feast.
Read Acts 2:37-47 to see what can happen when
people become suddenly aware of their deep need
for God's forgiveness through Jesus. How did the
people respond? What actions indicated their
great love for God and a joyful response to Him?

FORGIVENESS WITHIN COMMUNITY

Matthew 18:21-35

"HAVE YOU GIVEN YOURSELF permission to be angry at each other?"

Mark and Lauren were surprised at their marriage counselor's question. Their answer was a big, fat "Nope!" Anger? Wasn't that ungodly for people who were supposed to love each other? Couldn't they just say sorry and move on?

But after two months of feeling stuck in the counseling process, the couple realized that working so hard to *not* feel angry over their grievances was keeping them from being honest about the pain and grief they caused each other. Repeated sins toward those we love cause real pain that should not be ignored. Once Mark and Lauren understood that, they had a choice to make: either embrace a spirit of forgiveness while working toward change, or allow that pain to keep them stuck and increasingly distant.[1]

Like in a marriage, patterns of sin within a close-knit community can create feelings of betrayal and bitterness instead of compassion and forgiveness. Jesus did not gloss over that reality. In Matthew 18-20, He expounded on what scholars label "the Community Prescription," a how-to manual for His beloved church. These chapters help us understand what it looks like to be Kingdom representatives, proclaiming the gospel with words and walking it out "as a family of faith characterized by humility, purity, accountability, discipline, reconciliation, restoration, and forgiveness."[2] When Jesus gave instructions about how to respond to a fellow believer's sin (Matthew 18:15-20), the apostle Peter brought up the important issue of forgiveness.

1. Read Matthew 18:21-35. What questions did Peter ask? What details about his questions catch your attention?

_____

_____

_____

_____

_____

_____

_____

_____

_____

_____

_____

_____

Michael J. Wilkins writes, "The teaching within Judaism (based on Amos 1:3; 2:6; Job 33:29, 30) is that three times was enough to show a forgiving spirit. Rabbinic Judaism recognized that repeat offenders may not really be repenting at all. . . .

"Peter's question appears to be following in that line, wondering how many times he should forgive a person who repeatedly sins against him. His offer to forgive the person seven times, more than double the above-mentioned statements, is magnanimous, reflecting a desire for completeness that the number seven usually evokes. But he wonders whether this is where the limit should be drawn on his generosity of spirit."[3]

2. Jesus gave both a short answer and a longer answer to Peter's inquiry. What details of His answers do you notice? How does the longer parable flesh out His first statement?

_____

_____

_____

_____

_____

_____

_____

_____

_____

_____

_____

3. In His immediate answer (Matthew 18:22), Jesus chose a number many times larger than seven—either seventy-seven or seventy times seven, depending on how various early manuscripts rendered this saying. How might the large difference between Peter's number and Jesus' number have helped shift the disciples' perspective on forgiveness?

_____

_____

_____

_____

_____

_____

_____

4. In Matthew 18:23-35, Jesus expanded His answer through a parable that likened an aspect of God's Kingdom to part of life in their cultural context (see Matthew 13:24-52; Mark 4:26-34; Luke 13:18-21). How did Jesus use another large gap in numbers to make a point?

Discussing the ten thousand talents owed by the first servant to the king, Wilkins writes that by modern equivalents, "the man owes at least two and half billion dollars" while the second servant in the story owes "just a little over four thousand dollars, a pittance in comparison." The audience would have grasped that "the hyperbole of the parable [was] dramatic."[4]

_____

_____

_____

_____

_____

_____

_____

_____

_____

5. Jesus told His listeners that the king "wanted to settle accounts with his servants" (Matthew 18:23). How does this framing help us understand the nature of sin? What attribute(s) of God's nature does this settling of accounts suggest?

_____

_____

_____

_____

_____

_____

_____

_____

_____

6. In Matthew 18:27, the king responded to the servant's plea for patience. He "took pity on him, canceled the debt and let him go." What attribute(s) of God's nature does this response suggest?

_____

_____

_____

_____

_____

_____

_____

_____

_____

_____

_____

7. With the next scene, Jesus signaled His audience to look for a contrast: "But when that servant went out" (Matthew 18:28). What would have been the reasonable, expected actions of someone who had just been forgiven billions in debt? What do the first servant's subsequent actions reveal about his character and his heart?

_____

_____

_____

_____

_____

_____

_____

Craig Keener comments: "When poor crops or other circumstances forced a ruler to forgive taxes, he did so with the understanding that his people would respect his benevolence. If he released his subordinate ministers' debts, they in turn must release the debts of those indebted to them. This principle was widely known, and the first servant should have understood it . . . ; but as we have seen, this servant is a fool."[5]

8. In the final scene (Matthew 18:31-34), Jesus painted an even more dramatic settling of accounts between the king and the unforgiving servant, including a stark sentence of imprisonment and torture for the original huge debt. Scholars suggest the servant's lack of transformation and resulting punishment indicates the servant had "failed to embrace the principle of grace" from his master.[6] How does this parable point to the enormity of what Jesus would later do on the cross and the gift of grace offered to those who believe? How has freely accepting God's grace and forgiveness transformed your life?

_____

_____

_____

_____

_____

_____

_____

_____

Both Peter (Matthew 18:21) and Jesus (Matthew 18:35) use familial language in this parable. The Greek term *adelphos*, translated "brother or sister," increasingly became the term early Christians used to characterize "a fellow-believer, united to another by the bond of affection . . . constituting as it were but a single family."[7] The word *syndoulos*, meaning "fellow servant,"[8] also appears four times in this parable, emphasizing a community of those serving the same king. Though there are also broader applications, this teaching has particular implications for actions and attitudes within the body of Christ.

9. In a less dramatic sense, how might holding on to unforgiveness temporarily "imprison" believers though not affect their eternal security? What did Jesus offer as the prescription (Matthew 18:35)?

_____

_____

_____

_____

_____

_____

_____

_____

_____

_____

_____

10. What are the ways unforgiveness affected the community of fellow servants within the parable?

_____

_____

_____

_____

_____

_____

_____

_____

_____

_____

11. In what ways have you seen unforgiveness affect Christ's family, the church?

_____

_____

_____

_____

_____

_____

_____

_____

_____

_____

_____

12. How can fellow believers help each other foster a spirit of forgiveness and compassion both within and outside of our community?

_____

_____

_____

_____

_____

_____

_____

_____

_____

_____

_____

Your Response

While Jesus does not equate forgiveness with ignoring wrongdoing (see Matthew 18:15-20), He does call His followers to be transformed by His mercy and grace so that we constantly operate in a spirit of forgiveness toward others. Where is the Holy Spirit prompting you to move toward someone with forgiveness? If you are finding this difficult, which of your brothers or sisters in Christ could you talk to and ask for support in prayer?

For Further Study

Read Colossians 3:12-14. How are believers meant to be "clothed," both in their spiritual attitudes and in their actions toward one another? Why did the apostle Paul say this? How have you experienced these actions and attitudes from Christ recently? How does this realization prompt you to extend the same attitudes and actions toward another person this week?

THE LIFESTYLE OF FORGIVENESS

Romans 12:1-2, 9-21

CIVIL RIGHTS PIONEER AND Christian minister John M. Perkins has spent a lifetime calling the American church to lament racial injustice and promoting healing and reconciliation within the church and beyond. "Forgiveness," he contends, "is the linchpin of reconciliation."[1] However, he understands that forgiving, especially forgiving enemies, can be difficult. As a Black child growing up in racially segregated Mississippi, Perkins experienced ridicule, mistreatment, and discrimination. When he moved to California, interacting with several white people who offered him respect helped him "shed the wall of unforgiveness and distrust [of white people in general] that held my heart captive." But, he wrote, "I continued to harbor unforgiveness in my heart for whites in Mississippi." This "selective forgiveness," as he called it, came to the forefront for him when, upon returning to Mississippi, he was arrested and brutally beaten by authorities for his role in a peaceful protest. He faced a choice at that moment: Would he respond to God's call to forgive his enemies when revenge and hatred seemed like a reasonable response? He later wrote,

> Revenge seemed fair and right . . . but love was the only way pleasing to God. I'm grateful to God because He kept me from making foolish decisions [to retaliate] that would have most likely meant my life, and possibly the life of my family. . . . I owe a debt of gratitude to God for overwhelming my fleshly desire for revenge and hate and giving me His supernatural grace of forgiveness.[2]

The ability to move forward through forgiveness became the foundation for decades of reconciliation work over the rest of his life.

How could John Perkins forgive those who had no desire to be forgiven nor any remorse for their actions? He pointed to the work of God within him, to power beyond human will, and to examples of others in Scripture who were likewise empowered to forgive. Jesus asked God to forgive His crucifiers (Luke 23:34). The disciple Stephen similarly interceded for those stoning him to death (Acts 7:60). Paul and Silas, who had an opportunity to escape a Philippian prison cell, instead stayed to prevent their jailer from committing suicide. Their actions turned an enemy into a follower of Jesus (Acts 16:27-28).

We are called to become people who not only embrace God's forgiveness and extend it to fellow believers but also are agents of forgiveness and reconciliation in a desperate world. How? Paul's words in Romans 12 offer us a blueprint.

---

1. Read Romans 12:1-2, 9-21. Which key words and phrases catch your attention? Why do they stand out to you?

2. What kind of internal change(s) does Romans 12:1-2 say must happen in the lives of believers? How do these verses set the stage for the list of outward behaviors and attitudes listed in Romans 12:9-21?

_____

_____

_____

_____

_____

_____

_____

_____

_____

_____

3. In verses 9-21, which of the actions or attitudes focus more on interactions within the community of believers? Which ones focus more on outsiders?

_____

_____

_____

_____

_____

_____

_____

_____

_____

_____

Douglas Moo comments that the opening phrase in this passage may benefit from a more word-for-word translation to set up the remainder of the passage. He writes: "The Greek behind the NIV's 'Love must be sincere' has no verb; a very literal rendering would be 'the love sincere.' Supplying an imperative verb [of command] (as almost all the translations do) is not necessarily wrong, but it obscures the fact that these words seem to be a heading for the rest of the passage. It is as if Paul gives a definition: 'Love that is sincere will be . . .'" The list of instructions then shows believers how to avoid "love that is mere 'play-acting' if they put into practice the commands that follow."[3]

4. How did Paul characterize believers' responses to evil and good in Romans 12:9?

_____

_____

_____

_____

_____

_____

_____

_____

_____

_____

5. Other translations use the words *abhor* (ESV) or *detest* (CSB) for this response to evil. How might verses 14, 17, and 20-21 suggest that the response to evil does not include hating, abhorring, or detesting people?

_____

_____

_____

_____

_____

_____

_____

_____

_____

_____

_____

6. Focusing on Romans 12:14-17, what kinds of actions might be involved in carrying out the commands to "bless and do not curse" and to avoid "repay[ing] anyone evil for evil"?

_____

_____

_____

_____

_____

_____

_____

_____

_____

7. Read Matthew 5:43-45. What does Jesus teach about God's character and how He desires His children to illustrate that character?

_____

_____

_____

_____

_____

_____

_____

_____

_____

_____

Moo comments: "These similarities suggest that Paul is quoting Jesus' teaching here. In fact, Paul shows more dependence on Jesus' [recorded] teaching in this part of Romans than he does anywhere else in his letters. The way he weaves references to that teaching into his own exhortations without specifically citing Jesus is typical of the way early Christians absorbed Jesus' words into their own ethical tradition. Like Jesus, Paul calls on us to turn the other cheek, displaying a love for others that goes far beyond the normal boundaries of human love."[4]

8. What connections do you notice between Jesus' teaching and Paul's?

_____

_____

_____

_____

_____

_____

_____

_____

_____

_____

_____

9. Romans 12:18-21 offers even more detailed instructions on interacting with those outside the community of believers, which would have included those actively persecuting these early Christians. What encouragement does God offer in Romans 12:19 to those who choose to practice loving actions toward enemies?

_____

_____

_____

_____

_____

_____

_____

_____

_____

10. What does Romans 12:19 suggest about God's concern for justice?

_____

_____

_____

_____

_____

_____

_____

_____

_____

_____

_____

11. How might Christians "hate what is evil; cling to what is good" (Romans 12:9) in their interactions with their culture so that they express not only God's justice and holiness but also His mercy and forgiveness?

N. T. Wright comments: "This [passage on treatment of enemies] brings us to the question of whether it is possible to forgive someone who isn't sorry. . . . This passage seems to indicate that, though when someone isn't sorry there is no chance of full reconciliation, it is not only possible but actually commanded that we should rid ourselves of any desire for revenge. Instead, we should actually go out of our way to do positive, uncalled-for acts of kindness to those who have wronged us. That, in turn, may lead them at least to remorse (that is probably what the reference to 'burning coals' in verse 20, quoting Proverbs 25.21, is all about), or even to **repentance** and thereby to reconciliation."[5]

_____

_____

_____

_____

_____

_____

_____

_____

_____

_____

_____

12. Paul illustrates sincere love (Romans 12:9) with a series of actions, exhorting believers that love is not merely a feeling but something to be outwardly demonstrated. Consider someone in your life who holds an opposing or combative viewpoint. What would a forgiving posture toward that person look like?

_____

_____

_____

_____

_____

_____

_____

_____

13. What, if any, changes would be necessary to embody Romans 12:18—"If it is possible, as far as it depends on you, live at peace"—with that person?

_____

_____

_____

_____

_____

_____

_____

_____

_____

_____

14. What changes are needed for the larger church to embody peace and mercy to outsiders? How might that lifestyle of forgiveness open more opportunities for sharing the gospel?

Your Response

Even if we do not yet experience loving and forgiving feelings toward those who oppose us or have wronged us, we can rid ourselves of the need to seek vengeance—that is, we can forgive the relational debt those people have created and leave the matter in God's hands. In some cases it would be unwise, impractical, or dangerous to be reconciled. But what would it look like not to wish harm on those who have harmed us (Romans 12:14) or not to repay evil for evil (Romans 12:17)? What actions would demonstrate a choice to overcome evil with good (Romans 12:21)?

For Further Study

Read Acts 16:16-34. How were Paul and Silas treated by the authorities and why? What does verse 25 say the two men were doing, despite their circumstances, and who was listening to them? How did Paul and Silas choose to respond to their jailer, someone who could be considered their enemy, and what was the outcome? How might this encourage believers to seek a broader perspective on how they interact with the world around them?

NOTES

INTRODUCTION

1. Sharon Risher with Sherri Wood Emmons, *For Such a Time as This: Hope and Forgiveness after the Charleston Massacre* (Saint Louis: Chalice Press, 2019).
2. United Nations, "The Justice and Reconciliation Project in Rwanda," 2012, https://www.un.org/en/preventgenocide/rwanda/pdf/bgjustice.pdf.
3. Kirsten Weir, "Forgiveness Can Improve Mental and Physical Health," *Monitor on Psychology* 48, no. 1 (January 2017), https://www.apa.org/monitor/2017/01/ce-corner.

SESSION ONE—FORGIVENESS IN THE KINGDOM OF GOD

1. Corrie ten Boom, "Guideposts Classics: Corrie ten Boom on Forgiveness," *Guideposts*, January 6, 2023, https://guideposts.org/positive-living/guideposts-classics-corrie-ten-boom-forgiveness.
2. Craig S. Keener, *Matthew*, The IVP New Testament Commentary Series (Downers Grove, IL: IVP, 1997), 102.
3. Michael J. Wilkins, *Matthew*, The NIV Application Commentary (Grand Rapids, MI: Zondervan, 2004), 277.
4. Wilkins, *Matthew*, 279–80.

SESSION TWO—THE GOD WHO FORGIVES

1. Warren W. Wiersbe, *Be Delivered: Finding Freedom by Following God*, "BE" Commentary Series: Exodus (Colorado Springs: David C. Cook, 1998), 200.
2. Peter Enns, *Exodus*, The NIV Application Commentary (Grand Rapids, MI: Zondervan, 2000), 583.
3. Spiros Zodhiates, *Hebrew-Greek Key Word Study Bible—ESV*, ed. by Warren Baker (Chattanooga, TN: AMG, 2013), 1853.
4. Zodhiates, *Hebrew-Greek Key Word Study*, 1889.
5. Zodhiates, *Hebrew-Greek Key Word Study*, 1701.
6. "Exodus 34," study note 16, *NET Bible*, accessed November 11, 2022, https://netbible.org/bible/Exodus+34.
7. Martha Henriques, "Can the Legacy of Trauma Be Passed Down the Generations?" BBC Future, March 26, 2019, https://www.bbc.com/future/article/20190326-what-is-epigenetics.

Notes

SESSION THREE—FORESHADOWING FORGIVENESS
1. Details changed to protect privacy; story shared with permission.
2. William D. Mounce, ed., *Mounce's Complete Expository Dictionary of Old and New Testament Words* (Grand Rapids, MI: Zondervan, 2006), 44.
3. Mounce, *Mounce's Complete Expository Dictionary*, 45.
4. Michael F. Bird, *Evangelical Theology: A Biblical and Systematic Introduction*, 2nd ed. (Grand Rapids, MI: Zondervan Academic, 2020), 771–72.
5. N. T. Wright, *Hebrews for Everyone* (Louisville: Westminster John Knox, 2004), 107–8.

SESSION FOUR—THE GOSPEL OF FORGIVENESS
1. Details changed to protect privacy; story shared with permission.
2. Darrell L. Bock, *Luke*, The NIV Application Commentary (Grand Rapids, MI: Zondervan, 1996), 596.
3. As quoted in Barry J. Beitzel, *The New Moody Atlas of the Bible* (Chicago: Moody, 2009), 228.
4. Bock, *Luke*, 593.
5. David Crowther, "Luke," *Lexham Context Commentary: New Testament*, ed. Douglas Mangum (Bellingham, WA: Lexham Press, 2020), Luke 23:34. Accessed online at https://www.logos.com/context-commentary.
6. Warren W. Wiersbe, *The Bible Exposition Commentary*, New Testament, vol. 1 (Wheaton, IL: Victor Books, 2001), 275.
7. Bock, *Luke*, 599.

SESSION FIVE—REPENTING AND RECEIVING FORGIVENESS
1. E. Randolph Richards and Brandon J. O'Brien, *Misreading Scripture with Western Eyes: Removing Cultural Blinders to Better Understand the Bible* (Downers Grove, IL: IVP Books, 2012), 120–28.
2. Derek Kidner, *Psalms 1–72: An Introduction and Commentary*, vol. 15 of Tyndale Old Testament Commentaries (Downers Grove, IL: IVP, 1973), 212.
3. Tremper Longman III, *Psalms*, Tyndale Old Testament Commentaries, vol. 15–16 (Downers Grove, IL: IVP Academic, 2014), 219.
4. Longman, *Psalms*, 220.
5. Kidner, *Psalms 1–72*, 209, 211.

SESSION SIX—THE RESPONSE OF THE FORGIVEN
1. Darrell L. Bock, *Luke*, The NIV Application Commentary (Grand Rapids, MI: Zondervan, 1996), 218.
2. "Faith Lessons: Message in a Bottle (Luke 7)," interview with archaeologist and provost of The Bible Seminary, Dr. Scott Stripling, May 23, 2022, https://podcasts.apple.com/us/podcast/faith-lessons-message-in-a-bottle-luke-7/id1495569127?i=1000563292109.
3. J. D. Douglas and Merrill C. Tenney, eds., "Money," *Zondervan Illustrated Bible Dictionary* (Grand Rapids, MI: Zondervan, 2011), 967–69.
4. David Crowther, "Luke," *Lexham Context Commentary: New Testament*, ed. Douglas Mangum (Bellingham, WA: Lexham Press, 2020), Luke 7:36-50. Accessed online at https://www.logos.com/context-commentary.
5. Bock, *Luke*, 220.

SESSION SEVEN—FORGIVENESS WITHIN COMMUNITY

1. Details changed to protect privacy; story shared with permission.
2. Michael J. Wilkins, *Matthew*, The NIV Application Commentary (Grand Rapids, MI: Zondervan, 2004), 611.
3. Wilkins, *Matthew*, 622.
4. Wilkins, *Matthew*, 623–24.
5. Craig S. Keener, *Matthew*, The IVP New Testament Commentary Series (Downers Grove, IL: IVP, 1997), 292.
6. Keener, *Matthew*, 292.
7. Thayer's Greek Lexicon, Strong's G80, https://www.blueletterbible.org/lexicon/g80/kjv/tr/0-1.
8. Thayer's Greek Lexicon, Strong's G4889, https://www.blueletterbible.org/lexicon/g4889/kjv/tr/0-1.

SESSION EIGHT—THE LIFESTYLE OF FORGIVENESS

1. John M. Perkins, *One Blood: Parting Words to the Church on Race and Love* (Chicago: Moody, 2018), 99.
2. Perkins, *One Blood*, 108–9.
3. Douglas J. Moo, *Romans*, The NIV Application Commentary (Grand Rapids, MI: Zondervan, 2000), 409.
4. Moo, *Romans*, 411.
5. N. T. Wright, *Paul for Everyone: Romans, Part Two*, The New Testament for Everyone (Louisville: Westminster John Knox, 2004), 80.

LifeChange

A NAVPRESS BIBLE STUDY SERIES

LifeChange Bible studies train you in good Bible study practices even as you enjoy a robust and engaging Bible study experience. Learn the skill as you study the Word. There is a study for every book of the Bible and relevant topics.

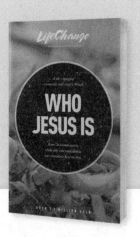

MAKE DISCIPLESHIP
A LIFESTYLE

THE 2:7 SERIES...
Discipleship training with a proven track record

DESIGN FOR DISCIPLESHIP...
Over 7 million sold

THE WAYS OF THE ALONGSIDER.....................................
For small groups, classes, or one-on-one discipling